QUIPNOTES
ABOUT DADS

by
Barbara Birenbaum

PEARTREE®

Published by
PEARTREE®
P.O. Box 14533
Clearwater, Florida 33766-4533
USA

Copyright 2003
ISBN: 0935343-083

Printed in the United States of America
10 9 8 7 6 5 4 3 2 1

CIP Data
Birenbaum, Barbara
  Quipnotes about dads / by Barbara Birenbaum
  p.cm.
    1. Fathers—Quotations, maxims, etc.
    2. Fatherhood--Quotations, maxims, etc.
    3. Fathers —Anecdotes. I. Title.

PN6084.F3 B57 2003   2002025284
306.874'2--dc21

Contents

Introduction

Dads are called by many names - Father, Dad, Daddy, Pop, Poppa and Papa. No matter what name is given to Dads, each Dad is special around the world.

*Dedicated to my Dad
and my husband who is also a Dad*

Dedicated to all the Dads of the world
who join together with insight and under-
standings that only Dads could discern.

About Dads . . .

$\mathcal{D}$ads become dads when children are born!

*D*ads find children
an investment,
hoping for the rewards
of their efforts.

Dads are
forward-looking,
not knowing what
to expect.

Dads have a built in
sixth sense,
plus more in reserve.

Dads spend a lifetime experiencing children.

*D*ads bring balance
to the highs and lows
of living.

*D*ads have a
wealth of experience just
waiting to be tapped.

*D*ads become
well-schooled in
children's behavior.

*D*ads work behind the
scene in your behalf.

*D*ads have a clear
picture of who you
are without getting
hung up on it.

$\mathcal{D}$ads come from behind
to encourage
your going forward.

*D*ads take great pride
watching their little
offspring become
individuals.

Dads helpful hints . . .

With allowance comes choices.

*L*ook out for
yourself before others
must look out for you!

*W*ork on your
manners as much as
your career.

A wallflower never
grows friends.

*S*elf-esteem
comes from within.

If you think you can
outsmart Dad,
try someone else.

If you don't want advice,
expect it anyhow.

Keep your life in focus to
know who you are.

$\mathcal{E}$nergize your mind
by learning something
new every day.

*C*ultivate friendships
to enrich your garden
of living.

If you wonder about life,
it is waiting to be
discovered.

Investing in yourself . . .

Living takes an outlay of investing in yourself.

$\mathcal{B}$alance your finances
and your selfhood.

*L*ife is more
complicated than the
stock market.

*L*ife has gyrations that
swing from high to low
and back again.

Make a living trust
between
you and yourself!

$\mathcal{D}$iversify your portfolio
of involvement
with and for others.

*T*he PE ratio of
accomplishment should
include Personal Endeavor.

*M*ultiply your interest in human causes.

$\mathcal{L}$et others profit from
your knowledge.

$\mathcal{D}$on't ask for anything
you can gain yourself!

Value-added
talents are to share
with others.

*P*atience is an
intangible asset acquired
with maturity.

$\mathcal{Y}$our net worth
is a measure of your
personhood over
a lifetime.

$\mathcal{B}$onding with Dads . . .

*D*ads bond with children,
hoping for some measure
of redemption.

Dads provide a safety
net for children.

*D*ads provide checks
and balances between your
wants and needs.

*D*ads measure your
growth by maturity.

*D*ads find children an investment for life.

*D*ads are as secure as
safety deposit boxes.

*D*ads have your
interest at heart,
even when not around.

ads profit from
your being.

Dads can be counted on
when least expected.

*D*ads invest in a
lifetime of learning.

*D*ads take into
account that all
children are special.

$\mathcal{A}$dvice from Dads . . .

*S*tand tall,
but bend to get the
cooperation of others.

If you live in a box,
make sure it has
windows and a door.

$\mathcal{A}$n ego can stand in
the way of the self.

If you insist on
being "cool," make sure
others have a fan.

*E*njoy what you do
and do what you enjoy.

In play with others,
look for harmony.

*I*n a world turned
upside-down,
keep your head on
your shoulders.

If you want to conform,
seek those who
are like-minded.

Like it or not,
you are who you are.

If you look
forward to tomorrow,
plan for today!

$\mathcal{F}$ishing with Dads . . .

*D*ads know
life is like fishing . . .
sometimes the best
comes last.

*D*ads know
life is like fishing. . .
never know what's
on the line.

*D*ads know
life is like fishing . . .
hope for a big catch,
but thankful for a nibble.

*D*ads know
life is like fishing . . .
getting nibbles before
a big bite.

*D*ads know
life is like fishing . . .
the lure attracts
temptation.

*D*ads know
life is like fishing . . .
reel in the opportunities
at hand.

*D*ads know
life is like fishing . . .
a game of skill in the
waters of chance.

*D*ads know
life is like fishing . . .
certainty is left to
the unknown.

*D*ads know
life is like fishing . . .
experiences are cast in
the waters of time.

*D*ads know
life is like fishing . . .
wait patiently like anglers
to see what happens.

*D*ads know
life is like fishing . . .
get hooked from the
beginning.

*D*ads know
life is like fishing . . .
cast toward a goal that
may not be in sight.

*D*ads know
life is like fishing . . .
a skillful art learned
over a lifetime.

*D*ads know
life is like fishing . . .
a big splash -
therein lies hope!

$\mathcal{D}$ads seem to know . . .

*D*ads seem to know children cannot walk through life alone.

*D*ads seem to know
when to let you wade or
swim on your own.

Dads seem to know
who you are no matter how
you grow and change.

*D*ads understand that
children must find
their own direction and
course in life.

*D*ads seem to know
when to pick the time
for lectures or laughter.

*D*ads know how
to ask a question to get
many answers.

$\mathcal{D}$ads seem to know
what you are
up to without their
being around.

*D*ads seem to know
the difference between
what you say and
what you do.

Dads realize children
rise to their own level
of personhood.

*D*ads realize children
confront currents
of unrest as they grow.

$\mathcal{D}$ads understand that
children grow up
with or without
their permission.

*W*hat's cooking with
Dads . . .

*D*ads watch children
stir up mischief.

Dads season food for thought by caring.

Dads are like
pressure-cookers,
often letting off steam.

*D*ads are the salt of the
earth and other
seasonings, too.

Dads know
what's brewing,
without a pot.

*D*ads know
if you can dish it out,
be prepared to eat
your words.

*D*ads concoct meals,
making a lot from
a little.

ads enjoy serving
individual portions
of love to children.

*D*ads waste not and recycle everything!

*D*ads create meals
out of chaos.

*D*ads indulge
children's craving,
hoping it feeds their
appetite for
future endeavor.

*D*ads offer
children a smorgasbord,
so they can make
choices in life.

Dads find children
the dessert of life,
while enjoying
other courses of living.

Coaching with Dads . . .

*D*ads go to bat for children who might otherwise strike out.

*D*ads may set the rules,
but children play
their own game of life.

*D*ads hope you
roll spares down
the alley of striving.

*T*ackle problems as
they arise,
each in its own way.

*T*ouchdowns of success
come with team effort.

*O*ne action creates
another on the
field of endeavor.

*P*ut problems in a bedroll
and camp near paths
of solutions.

*G*rowing up comes
in cycles,
some just pedal faster
than others.

$\mathcal{V}$olley choices across
the net of experience.

*T*hrow fear beyond reach,
where it can do little harm.

*W*hen you are thrown
a curve ball,
work around it.

*W*hen you are
thrown a spin ball,
keep control.

*W*hen you are
thrown a fast ball,
take time to react.

If you bunt your way through life, you may miss other choices.

*I*t takes putters and irons
to propel long drives
toward goals.

*G*iving up while you're
ahead never gets
anyone further,
faster.

Logic from Dads . . .

*T*he illogic of today
may become the logic
of tomorrow.

*D*ads learn from children what they have yet to understand.

*G*o after your goals,
but keep a steady course.

*P*ursue your aspirations
within a framework
of reality.

*S*trike a balance
between your strengths
and limitations.

*H*elp others feel good
about themselves.

$\mathcal{K}$eep your life in focus
with a clear
image of yourself.

*D*ads follow
the course of your life
without a map.

Selfhood takes a
lifetime of living.

*A*rguments get you
nowhere with Dads who
have selective hearing.

*B*etter to know
who you are than
who you think you are.

*C*ommit the self
to challenge the future.

*S*ize up your options
and take stock
in your decisions.

Market yourself in a well-rounded package.

$\mathcal{F}$riends may
come and go,
but Dads are forever.

$\mathcal{W}$hat if . . .

If the future is
in your hands,
how come it's so difficult
to grasp?

If you are so
sure of yourself,
how come you seek
approval?

If you want to know
who you are,
just ask someone else.

If you think you know everything, just ask Dad.

If you have to ask
permission,
the answer is,
"No."

If you run out of time, get another watch.

If you are driven
to achieve,
make sure you have
a license.

If everything is
by the numbers,
who's keeping score?

If life is a puzzle,
who moves the pieces?

If thinking is an art,
how is it acquired?

$\mathcal{D}$ads workshops . . .

*D*ads have workbenches
to help children
work out their kinks.

If you plan on a power play with Dad, know the tools he uses.

*D*ads may hammer a
point across without
pounding nails.

$\mathcal{D}$ads use a lathe
to reshape relationships.

*D*ads help to sand down
rough edges of experience.

*D*ads know
children are pliable.

$\mathcal{D}$ads get to the
nuts and bolts of issues.

*D*ads try to
straighten out children
who seem bent
out of shape.

*D*ads realize warped
ideas will dry up
with age.

*D*ads use goggles
to protect relationships.

$\mathcal{D}$ads try to wedge
logic into
children's thinking.

$\mathcal{D}$ads work
from all angles to get
your cooperation.

$\mathcal{D}$ads know life is built on experiences.

*D*ads are like carpenters,
with a workbench of tools
to meet children's needs.

Children measure up . . .

*D*ads believe children
will add up to something.

*D*ads figure out what
children have left behind.

*D*ads expect a
measure of cooperation.

*D*ads watch as you sum up your relationships.

*I*t doesn't take math to find solutions to your own problems.

*K*now how to discern parts from the whole in situations.

*F*ractions are pieces to the puzzle of life.

A standoff is like
a decimal point waiting
to be moved.

*R*ound to the highest
level your estimated
human worth.

You can count on Dad,
who can also count
on you.

*F*actor in your family
when expressing
feelings.

*C*ompound simple
thoughts to get
complex ideas.

*Y*ou are a composite
of a whole, constantly
in the making.

$\mathcal{D}$ivide your problems in
half to multiply
the positive outlook of
your efforts.

$\mathcal{R}$*elationships* . . .

*A*ll things average out in life.

ou are the sum of
your actions.

$\mathcal{Y}$ou are a fractional
equivalent of your
total being.

*O*nly you have the means
to balance extremes.

If you think you are a
square peg in a round hol
think of all the other
shapes you could be.

Only you can
confront the roots to
your problems.

*F*actor in all the
influences of your actions
before squaring off
a response.

$\mathscr{T}$he base is your
beginning, which then
akes a life of self identity.

$\mathcal{T}$he equations of relationships are often too complex to figure.

ea to shore with
Dads . . .

*D*ads are beacons
for those who have
lost their way.

*D*ads harbor no doubts
that each child
is special.

$\mathcal{D}$ads provide oars,
so children can paddle
their way through life.

Dads are like ham radios,
sending and receiving
messages.

*D*ads help you
dig through sand dunes
of difficulties.

*D*ads may not be in sight, but keep you in mind.

*D*ads watch as you
go in and out of
relationships like the tide

*D*ads are there for
children who get in
over their heads.

Dads crest the waves of frustration with children.

*D*ads toss out a safety
net for those caught in
an undertow.

*D*ads counter the
ebb and flow
of your moods with a
steady hand.

*D*ads catch the
undercurrents of
your feelings.

Dads harbor your
well-being without
a port.

*D*ads watch you sail
through currents
of experience.

Quipnotes about Dads . .

$\mathcal{D}$ads are like flashlights,
turned on when you want
them turned off.

If you expect Dad to be
there for you,
better give him directions.

"*T*his is your Father,"
means Dad is
really mad!

If you wait for Dad's reaction, get call-waiting.

*D*ads are
like the Internet,
on line all the time.

*D*ads come packaged
with patience for
children who try theirs.

Dads give generously
from their pockets
of love.

If you think Dads are from another planet, why are they so well-grounded?

If Dad watches over you, there must be a reason.

*D*ads may be
pushovers for allowance,
but hold children
accountable for their
spending.

If you think Dad was never there for you, he was probably looking out for your welfare.

*D*ads are good people
to start lives with.

A Dad called by any
other name,
must be someone else.

*W*hen God made Dads . . .

$\mathcal{H}$e didn't ask anyone
for permission.

*H*e created another lifeline.

*H*e knew Dad could accept his responsibility.

*H*e had faith in his hidden talents of parenthood.

$\mathcal{H}$e knew every child
needed one.

*H*e gave him a contract renewable through life.

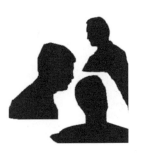

*H*e was proud of
his handiwork.

*H*e preserved the
mold for eternity.

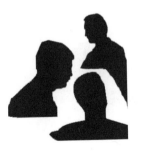

$\mathcal{H}$e blessed each
family with one.

*H*e made each Dad
different so children
would be unique.

$\mathcal{A}$ttuned to Dads . . .

*D*ads think surround
sound is created when
children are born.

*D*ads get used to
quadraphonic sound,
hearing multiple views
on everything.

$\mathcal{D}$ads are like CD's,
on track even
if you're not.

*D*ads advice is with you,
even if tuned out.

Dads are used to acoustics of living.

*D*ads find ways to keep
children on track.

*D*ads see situations with high intensity vision.

*D*ads often prefer
to reflect in pause mode
before reacting.

*D*ads and children
are attuned to one another
when least expected.

Tidbits and afterthoughts of Dads . . .

$\mathcal{D}$ads expect you to listen
even if they
have little to say!

Dads can forgive and
forget sooner than
you can remember
what happened.

*D*ads have patience
to explain things,
when you have little
patience to understand.

*D*ads who say nothing,
keep children
wondering why.

$\mathcal{D}$ads give and take without playing games.

*D*ads pass time waiting
for you to find yourself,
while you wait for
time to pass.

*D*ads share their lives with children who appreciate their value as adults.

*D*ads who allocate time,
try to apportion some to
enjoying children.

*D*ads get a reaction, even if it comes as a delayed response!

*D*ads are what others
can't be until they
become one.

Children often find Dads
everything they hoped for
and more!

$\mathcal{L}$et's face it,
Dads are a difficult
act to follow.

Look for other titles of this series

by Barbara Birenbaum

Quipnotes About Moms
Quipnotes About Aunts
Quipnotes About Uncles
Quipnotes About People

From PEARTREE ®